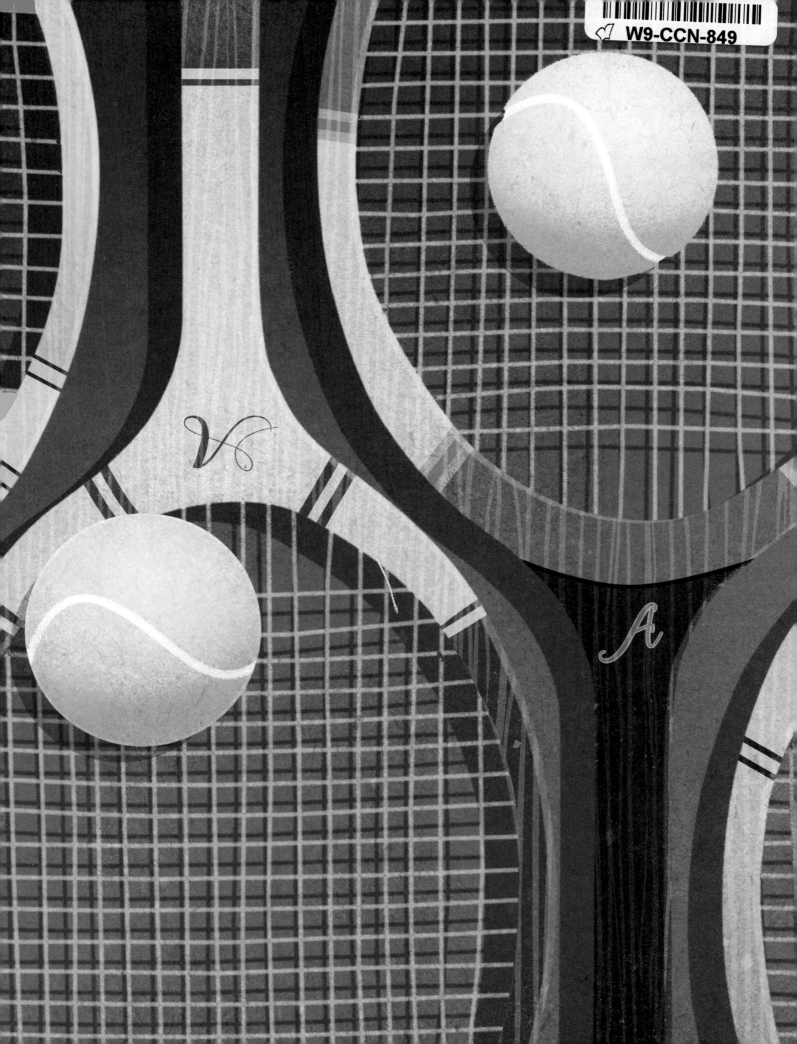
W9-CCN-849

ALTHEA
THE STORY OF TENNIS'

To my mom, Aunt Carole, and Wendi Gu
—M.R.

To my sister, Roberta
—L.F.

Balzer + Bray is an imprint of HarperCollins Publishers.

Althea Gibson: The Story of Tennis' Fleet-of-Foot Girl

Text copyright © 2020 by Megan Reid

Illustrations copyright © 2020 by Laura Freeman

All rights reserved. Manufactured in China.

No part of this book may be used or reproduced in any manner whatsoever without written permission except in the case of brief quotations embodied in critical articles and reviews. For information address HarperCollins Children's Books, a division of HarperCollins Publishers, 195 Broadway, New York, NY 10007.

www.harpercollinschildrens.com

Library of Congress Control Number: 2018968545

ISBN 978-0-06-285109-3

The artist used Adobe Photoshop to create the digital illustrations for this book.

Typography by Dana Fritts

19 20 21 22 23 SCP 10 9 8 7 6 5 4 3 2 1

❖

First Edition

GIBSON
FLEET-OF-FOOT GIRL

Written by
Megan Reid

Illustrated by
Laura Freeman

BALZER + BRAY
An Imprint of HarperCollinsPublishers

The championships at Wimbledon, England, were where the most famous tennis athletes in the world competed to be the best.

Sharp white collars.

Sharp white pleats.

Sharp white lines.

But in 1940s Harlem, the quickest, tallest, most fearless athlete was Althea Gibson.

At thirteen, Althea didn't know about Wimbledon, and she didn't care. When summer came and school let out, the only thing on her mind was this: the Play Streets up on 143rd.

For two months, the neighborhood's
streets were barricaded off, and kids
ruled the hot asphalt.
"Althea! Althea!"
Everywhere she went, they called
the fleet-of-foot girl to play.

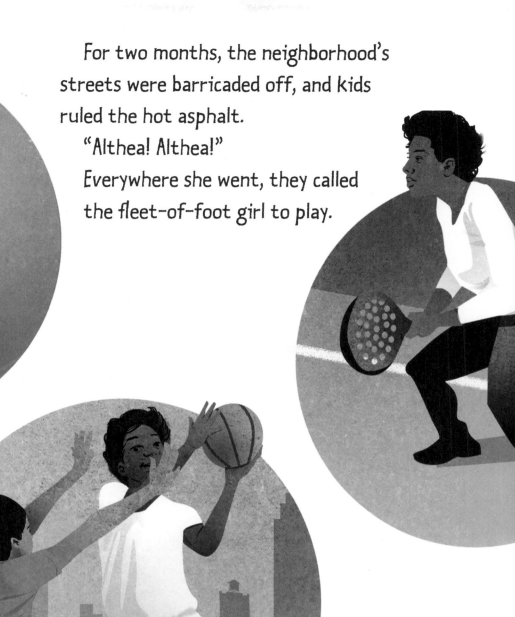

Althea played, all right. Stickball
with the boys, basketball with the
girls, paddle tennis with anyone and
everyone who would hit with her.

She reigned supreme. If she put her mind
to it, Althea was always the best.
At everything except sitting still.

summer was over and traffic returned to Harlem's busy streets, she still needed to move.

Althea heard about a place six blocks up where black folks could play tennis—the Cosmopolitan Tennis Club. She walked in like she already belonged, grabbed a ball and a racket, and started to swing.

Who is she? the grown-ups at the club asked. She
could sprint and turn and leap like a natural.
"I'm Althea Gibson," she announced, smiling widely.
"You should play with me."

She found her new Play Streets on the club's courts. She loved the way the balls cracked—*Pah!*—against her racket's taut strings. She started to spend more and more time at the Cosmopolitan. There, Althea wasn't just a scrappy, long-legged tomboy. No, she was pure talent. Pure force. The managers knew her family didn't have much money, so they let her do odd jobs in exchange for lessons.

Maybe, just maybe, the folks at the Cosmopolitan thought, *this fleet-of-foot girl could play tennis against the country's best.*

There was one big problem: Laws and white people's
prejudices kept black and brown Americans from claiming the
same rights to work, vote, buy property, and live freely. Black
people could play tennis in their own league, but never with
white people. Clubs like the Cosmopolitan were rare. Who could
challenge Althea when she had already beat everyone there?

Being the quickest, tallest, most fearless player in Harlem wasn't enough for Althea. She wanted to be a tennis champion. She started traveling for matches and training with other black players in the American Tennis Association.

She had a big serve and an even bigger personality.

She was so eager to prove herself that she wasn't always kind.

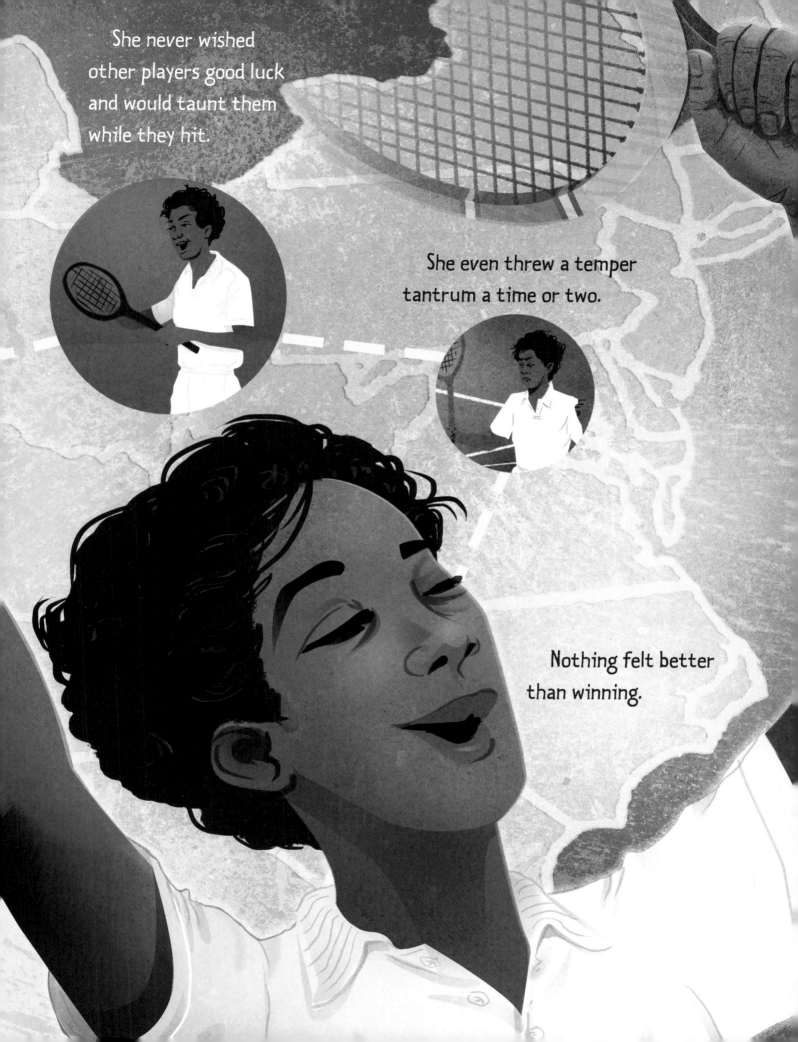

She never wished other players good luck and would taunt them while they hit.

She even threw a temper tantrum a time or two.

Nothing felt better than winning.

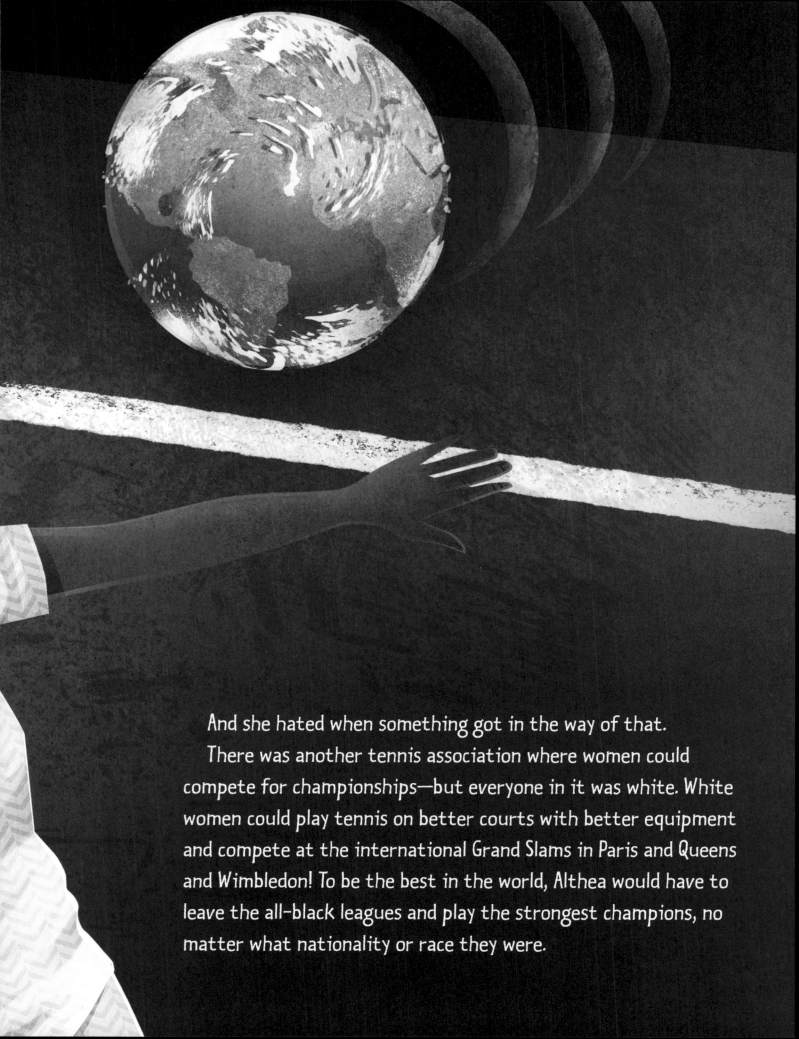

And she hated when something got in the way of that.

There was another tennis association where women could compete for championships—but everyone in it was white. White women could play tennis on better courts with better equipment and compete at the international Grand Slams in Paris and Queens and Wimbledon! To be the best in the world, Althea would have to leave the all-black leagues and play the strongest champions, no matter what nationality or race they were.

Journalists marveled at her wins and began to write about her in the newspapers. Famous players argued her cause. They saw that she deserved more.

And back in New York, kids still told stories about that girl Althea—how she'd beat anyone in netball and handball and fly though hopscotch so fast you couldn't even see her. A Harlem kid, like them!

Slowly, the world was changing. African Americans had been told they were "separate but equal" for too long. But Althea knew she could be more than equal—she could be the best.

Finally, in 1950, Althea was accepted to the
US championships.
    She lost her first set of matches, but she refused to quit.
By then, she had learned a little more about being a gracious
loser. "I don't mind getting beat. The more I am beaten, the
more I will learn," she said.

Sometimes she was lonely. In the locker rooms, Althea was left out of other players' inside jokes and secrets. She wasn't rich. She didn't look like them. She didn't play like them.

But when she charged the net, no one could doubt her confidence and power.

When the season ended, she still craved
the court—just like when autumn came and
the Play Streets' barricades were put away.
She couldn't just sit around. Althea was off
to travel the world!
Forehands in France,
ground strokes in Germany,
backhands in Burma,
serving in Sweden!

Althea just kept winning and winning. In Paris, she even became the first black person to win a Grand Slam.

But Althea had set her sights on claiming the silver trophy at Wimbledon, the biggest and best tournament of them all.

It was 1957, and the fleet-of-foot girl had earned it. For those two weeks in Wimbledon, Althea played better than ever. Her shots were cleaner; her volleys were quicker. Nothing was going to keep her away from the championship.

When she strode onto Centre Court to compete for the Wimbledon final, hers was the only black face in a sea of sharp white collars and sharp white pleats. So Althea focused on the grassy court's sharp white lines—just like the ones at the Cosmopolitan, or the ones she'd drawn with her chalk on the Play Streets. She took a deep breath and bounced the white tennis ball: one, two, three.

Almost before she knew it: game, set, match.

That year, Althea became the first-ever black person—
man or woman—to win a championship at Wimbledon.

And then in 1958,
she did it again.
The queen handed
Althea her prize.

She danced and sang with joy at the Wimbledon Champions Ball.

But best of all, back in New York that summer, they threw her a ticker-tape parade. "Althea! Althea!"

They cheered loudly for the quickest, tallest, most fearless girl Harlem had ever seen.

"I want the public to remember me
as they knew me. Strong, athletic,
smart, and healthy.... Remember me
strong and tough and quick,
fleet of foot and tenacious."

—Althea Gibson

AUTHOR'S NOTE

*A*s a child, I was often told I was "too much": too opinionated, too headstrong, too tall, too skinny, too black, too energetic to fit in. Maybe that's why I've always been fascinated by the stories of girls and women who were also told that their interests and goals made them "too much" for the society they lived in. My idols were Janet Reno, Michelle Kwan, and Dominique Dawes (not to mention Anne of Green Gables and Meg Murry)—but I wish I'd known Althea Gibson's story.

"I knew that I was an unusual, talented girl through the grace of God," Althea said. Others' opinions never stopped her confidence in her game.

I think that's because she never lost her sense of fun as she rose to the top. Althea came from humble roots as the daughter of a sharecropper in South Carolina, but she was a Harlem street kid through and through, curious and rowdy and full of life. But her life could be incredibly difficult. When she toured with the all-black American Tennis Association (ATA), she and her teammates were attacked with axes, threatened, and called hurtful names by spectators. When she mixed socially with the middle-class black bourgeoisie, Althea was told she was too "mannish" and unmannered to fit a feminine ideal.

But she kept her street-kid toughness—the confidence to be an opinionated, headstrong, tall, skinny, black, energetic young woman in the staid world of tennis. I think she was beautiful: Althea moved with a dancer's delicacy as she prepared for a backhand but dashed like a sprinter as her long arms and legs spanned the court. And she had a huge, amazing life after she retired from tennis. She was the first black woman to play golf professionally as part of the Ladies Professional Golf Association. She made her mark in Hollywood, wrote two books, and even recorded an album of her own.

Althea rarely spoke about her race or the struggles she experienced as the first black tennis player to make a major mark on the world stage. But no matter what she thought, the enormity of what she overcame can't be overstated, and just by existing in this world, she eased the way for future generations of great African American female players, like Venus and Serena Williams, Sloane Stephens, Madison Keys, and Zina Garrison.

In researching Althea's story, I was deeply touched by the extraordinary support she received from other women. Her tennis idol, Alice Marble, advocated for her after a young Althea saw her play. Her Jewish British tennis partner, Angela Buxton, became a friend, roommate, and coconspirator in lots of fun, and it was with Angela that Althea actually won her *first* Wimbledon title, for doubles tennis in 1956. (I chose to focus on Althea's headline-making singles win in 1957 in this book because it is seen as the more striking achievement, and she seemed to view it that way, too.) I'm so glad that Althea had safe places where she didn't need to be tough, even as she fought to earn the right to play tennis with the best.

In her memoir *I Always Wanted to Be Somebody* she said, "I want the public to remember me as they knew me. Strong, athletic, smart, and healthy. . . . Remember me strong and tough and quick, fleet of foot and tenacious." I hope this book does just that.

IMPORTANT DATES

1916—The all-black American Tennis Association (ATA) is founded.

August 25, 1927—Althea Gibson is born in Silver, South Carolina, to sharecropping cotton farmers.

1930—Althea and her family move up north to Harlem in New York City.

1939—At age twelve, Althea becomes New York City's women's paddle tennis champion.

1940—Althea's neighbors send her to the Cosmopolitan Tennis Club.

1941—Althea wins the very first tournament she enters in the ATA. She is fourteen years old.

1947—Althea wins the first of ten straight ATA national women's championship titles.

1949—Althea attends Florida A&M University on a full athletic scholarship.

August 22, 1950—Althea becomes the first black American to compete at the US national championships.

1951—Althea wins her first international championship, in Jamaica.

1956—Althea wins the women's singles title at the French Open. She is the first black athlete to win a Grand Slam event. She also wins the doubles title at Wimbledon with her friend Angela Buxton.

July 6, 1957—Althea wins the women's singles title at Wimbledon. She is the first champion to receive the trophy personally from Queen Elizabeth II.

1957—Althea is named Woman Athlete of the Year by the Associated Press.

1958—Althea wins the women's singles title at Wimbledon *again*! She is the only woman of color to win a major championship for fifteen years, and the only African American woman to win a major singles title for forty-three years, until Serena Williams wins the 1999 US Open.

1958—Althea publishes her first memoir, *I Always Wanted to Be Somebody*.

1963—At age thirty-six, Althea becomes the first black woman to golf in the Ladies Professional Golf Association.

1971—Althea is inducted into the International Tennis Hall of Fame.

1980—Althea is in the first class of athletes to be inducted into the International Women's Sports Hall of Fame, along with luminaries like Amelia Earhart.

1993—After medical emergencies, Althea is given hundreds of thousands of dollars from the international tennis community, demonstrating their respect and love for a former champion.

September 28, 2003—Althea dies after a series of health battles. She is buried in Orange, New Jersey, near the love of her life, Will Darben.

TO LEARN MORE ABOUT ALTHEA

Gray, Frances Clayton, and Yanick Rice Lamb. *Born to Win: The Authorized Biography of Althea Gibson*. Hoboken, NJ: Wiley, 2004.

Harris, Cecil, and Larryette Kyle-DeBose. *Charging the Net: A History of Blacks in Tennis from Althea Gibson and Arthur Ashe to the Williams Sisters*. Lanham, MD: Ivan R. Dee, 2007.

Miller, Rex, dir. *American Masters: Althea*. 2014; Arlington, VA: PBS, 2015, DVD.

Schoenfeld, Bruce. *The Match: Althea Gibson & Angela Buxton: How Two Outsiders—One Black, the Other Jewish—Forged a Friendship and Made Sports History*. New York: Amistad, 2004.

Thomas, Jr., Robert McG. "An Unlikely Champion." *New York Times*, September 29, 2003.

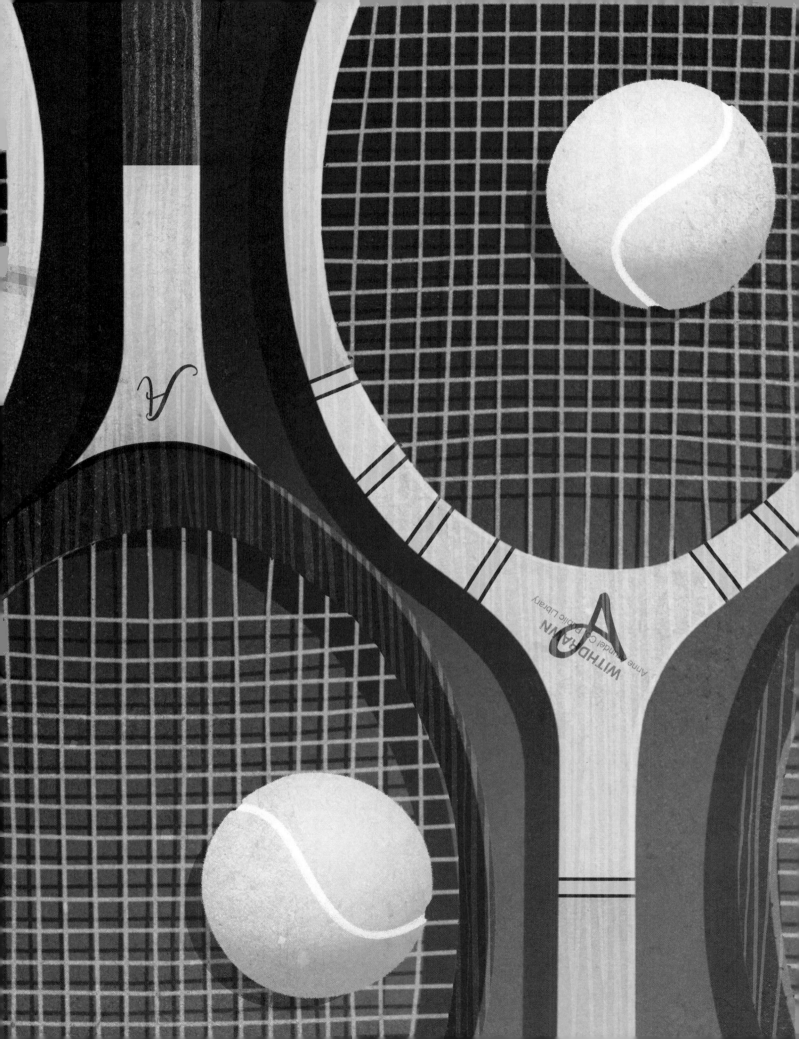

WITHDRAWN
Anne Arundel Co Public Library